# CONVERGE
### Bible Studies

# WOMEN OF THE BIBLE

Bible Studies

# WOMEN OF THE BIBLE

## JAMES A. HARNISH

Abingdon Press

Nashville

**WOMEN OF THE BIBLE**
**CONVERGE BIBLE STUDIES**

By James A. Harnish

Library of Congress Cataloging-in-Publication Data has been requested.

ISBN: 978-1-4267-7154-5

Series Editor: Shane Raynor

13 14 15 16 17 18 19 20 21 22 — 10 9 8 7 6 5 4 3 2 1

Manufactured in the United States of America

# CONTENTS

# ABOUT THE SERIES

*Converge* is a new series of topical Bible studies based on the Common English Bible translation. Each title in the *Converge* series consists of four studies based around a common topic or theme. *Converge* brings together a unique group of writers from different backgrounds, traditions, and age groups.

## HOW TO USE THESE STUDIES

*Converge* Bible studies can be used by small groups, classes, or individuals. Each study uses a simple format. For the convenience of the reader, the primary Scripture passages are included. In Insight and Ideas, the author of the study guide explores each Scripture passage, going deeper into the text and helping readers understand how the Scripture connects with the theme of the study. Questions are designed to encourage both personal reflection and group conversation. Some questions may not have simple answers. That's part of what makes studying the Bible so exciting.

Although Bible passages are included with each session, study participants may find it useful to have personal Bibles on hand for referencing other Scriptures. *Converge* studies are designed for use with the Common English Bible; but they work well with any modern, reliable translation.

## ONLINE EXTRAS

*Converge* studies are available in both print and digital formats. Each title in the series has additional components that are available online, including companion articles, blog posts, extra questions, sermon ideas, and podcasts.

To access the companion materials, visit

*http://www.MinistryMatters.com/Converge*

Thanks for using *Converge*!

# INTRODUCTION

I'm old enough to remember the 1968 commercial that declared, "You've come a long way, Baby!" Unfortunately, the advertisements for Virginia Slims cigarettes were so effective that our nation saw a significant increase in smoking among teenage girls who bought into the idea that it was a personal expression of a new era of freedom and power for women. It was the wrong product, but it was the right message.

Though we still have work to do, we have come a long way in affirming the unique strengths of women and liberating those strengths from the narrow confines of a male-dominated church culture.

I entered the ministry when the church was beginning to feel the influence of the feminist movement. The first women to be ordained as elders in our (United Methodist) annual conference are still colleagues and friends. The first associate pastor to serve with me was a woman who became my peer. Throughout ministry I've experienced the ways in which the church has changed because of the leadership and witness of women.

I am a husband, the father of two adult daughters, and the grandfather of one granddaughter. All these women continue to teach me more about being a man by being the strong, gifted, independent women they are. In short, I have been blessed and challenged by the faithful women with whom I share my life and ministry.

One of the gifts that women bring to the Christian community is a fresh awareness of the role of women in Scripture. Although the Bible was written in a patriarchal culture in which men get most of the lead roles, the action also moves forward through women—prophets and prostitutes, maidens and matrons, saints and sinners—who play a critical role in the drama of God's salvation. I was surprised to discover that there are 188 women whose names appear in the Bible, along with an unnumbered cast of unnamed women who play their role in the fulfillment of God's saving purpose.

Some of their names are familiar. Mary, the mother of Jesus, is engulfed in a sea of Roman Catholic piety and Christmas card nostalgia. Mary Magdalene gets movie star status in a near-voyeuristic fascination with her supposedly question-able past or the unlikely possibility that she was married to Jesus. Elizabeth has her moment on the stage each Advent by giving birth to John the Baptist in the geriatric ward while Zechariah stands by in stunned silence. Ruth is lauded for her loyalty to her mother-in-law and for becoming an ancestor of King David. Eve takes the blame for everything from sexual sin to pain in childbirth.

At the same time, some of the most intriguing women in Scripture are relatively unknown. I'll confess that I had never paid much attention to Abigail, who saved her people from war, or Deborah, who led her people into one. I'd had only a passing acquaintance with Lydia, whose home was the birthplace of the church in Philippi and whose business acumen provided the financial resources for Paul's missionary endeavors. Meeting them was like making a new acquaintance with some of the most fascinating people I had ever known.

This study grew out of a desire among the leaders of our congregation to discover how some of the women who made a difference in the Bible could make a difference in our lives today. It is rooted in biblical research, but it was informed by the insights of women who serve on our staff and in leadership in our congregation.

The women who are included in this four-session series are, to put it bluntly, some of my favorites. Each of them continues to surprise, challenge, and inspire me in ways that go beyond my expectations.

The Samaritan woman at the well moved me to a deeper awareness of the brokenness and spiritual thirst that are common to many of us. She also challenged all of us to be more transparent in offering the invitation, "Come and see."

Abigail drew me back to a fundamental commitment to Jesus' way of nonviolence that I had learned from Methodists in South Africa and that was demonstrated by a faithful woman in our congregation.

Deborah challenged me to search for a way to be both a faithful witness to the gospel and a patriotic heir to our national heritage. She also forced me to respond to one of the most persistent roadblocks people run into when they read the Old Testament.

I thought that I knew Mary Magdalene. But this time she broke free from my homiletical assumptions and pop culture portraits to become a model for a life of discipleship that leads through the cross to the new life of the Resurrection.

My hope is that this study will be the beginning of a new friendship with these women and others like them so that we will be drawn into a fresh awareness of what it means for all of us—men and women alike—to be more faithful disciples of Jesus Christ. By discovering the difference they make in the Bible we can discover the difference they can make for us.

We've come a long way, but we still have a long way to go.

# 1

# DEBORAH
## PASSIONATE PATRIOT

## SCRIPTURE
### JUDGES 4:1-24

¹After Ehud had died, the Israelites again did things that the Lord saw as evil. ²So the Lord gave them over to King Jabin of Canaan, who reigned in Hazor. The commander of his army was Sisera, and he was stationed in Harosheth-ha-goiim. ³The Israelites cried out to the Lord because Sisera had nine hundred iron chariots and had oppressed the Israelites cruelly for twenty years.

⁴Now Deborah, a prophet, the wife of Lappidoth, was a leader of Israel at that time. ⁵She would sit under Deborah's palm tree between Ramah and Bethel in the Ephraim highlands, and the Israelites would come to her to settle disputes. ⁶She sent word to Barak, Abinoam's son, from Kedesh in Naphtali and said to him, "Hasn't the Lord, Israel's God, issued you a command? 'Go and assemble at Mount Tabor, taking ten thousand men from the

people of Naphtali and Zebulun with you. [7]I'll lure Sisera, the commander of Jabin's army, to assemble with his chariots and troops against you at the Kishon River, and then I'll help you overpower him.'"

[8]Barak replied to her, "If you'll go with me, I'll go; but if not, I won't go."

[9]Deborah answered, "I'll definitely go with you. However, the path you're taking won't bring honor to you, because the LORD will hand over Sisera to a woman." Then Deborah got up and went with Barak to Kedesh. [10]He summoned Zebulun and Naphtali to Kedesh, and ten thousand men marched out behind him. Deborah marched out with him too.

[11]Now Heber the Kenite had moved away from the other Kenites, the descendants of Hobab, Moses' father-in-law, and had settled as far away as Elon-bezaanannim, which is near Kedesh.

[12]When it was reported to Sisera that Barak, Abinoam's son, had marched up to Mount Tabor, [13]Sisera summoned all of his nine hundred iron chariots and all of the soldiers who were with him from Harosheth-ha-goiim to the Kishon River. [14]Then Deborah said to Barak, "Get up! This is the day that the LORD has handed Sisera over to you. Hasn't the LORD gone out before you?" So Barak went down from Mount Tabor with ten thousand men behind him. [15]The LORD threw Sisera and all the chariots and army into a panic before Barak; Sisera himself got down from his chariot and fled

on foot. [16]Barak pursued the chariots and the army all the way back to Harosheth-ha-goiim, killing Sisera's entire army with the sword. No one survived.

[17]Meanwhile, Sisera had fled on foot to the tent of Jael, the wife of Heber the Kenite, because there was peace between Hazor's King Jabin and the family of Heber the Kenite. [18]Jael went out to meet Sisera and said to him, "Come in, sir, come in here. Don't be afraid." So he went with her into the tent, and she hid him under a blanket.

[19]Sisera said to her, "Please give me a little water to drink. I'm thirsty." So she opened a jug of milk, gave him a drink, and hid him again. [20]Then he said to her, "Stand at the entrance to the tent. That way, if someone comes and asks you, 'Is there a man here?' you can say, 'No.'"

[21]But Jael, Heber's wife, picked up a tent stake and a hammer. While Sisera was sound asleep from exhaustion, she tiptoed to him. She drove the stake through his head and down into the ground, and he died. [22]Just then, Barak arrived after chasing Sisera. Jael went out to meet him and said, "Come and I'll show you the man you're after." So he went in with her, and there was Sisera, lying dead, with the stake through his head.

[23]So on that day God brought down Canaan's King Jabin before the Israelites. [24]And the power of the Israelites grew greater and greater over Canaan's King Jabin until they defeated him completely.

## INSIGHT AND IDEAS

If you've ever been tempted to think that women are the "weaker sex," you've 1) never been with a woman in labor, and 2) you've never met a woman named Deborah. She was one tough woman who was strong enough to get the job done when the men around her were weak.

The year was 1125 B.C. The Israelites had been oppressed by King Jabin the Canaanite for twenty years while Sisera, the commander of his army, occupied the plain of Jezreel.

The Israelites were discouraged, depressed, and downhearted. Their leaders had lost the will to struggle against their oppressors. The people had settled into a servile life that was beneath what God intended for them. Their sense of their own identity as the covenant people had been dashed to smithereens under the weight of Sisera's occupation.

Enter Deborah. She was married to a man named Lappidoth. The only thing we know about him is that he married above himself. We meet Deborah under a palm tree where she served as a judge or counselor to the people.

My guess is that Deborah got sick and tired of listening to people describe the way they were suffering under Sisera's occupation. She confronted a leader named Barak with a rhetorical question: "Hasn't the Lord, Israel's God, issued you a command?" In no uncertain terms, she told him that God was directing him to take ten thousand troops to

Mount Tabor and lead the insurgency against Sisera. She even laid out the battle plan and promised that together they could overcome the occupation.

Barak wasn't convinced that this was such a great idea. With something less than undaunted courage, he replied, "If you'll go with me, I'll go; but if not, I won't go." That's not exactly what you call courageous leadership. Deborah told him not to worry. She would have his back. She promised, "I'll definitely go with you." But she also warned him that the honor of the victory over Sisera would go to a woman and not to him.

The conversation between Deborah and Barak reminded me of the way Shakespeare's Lady Macbeth tells her spineless husband, "Screw your courage to the sticking place and we'll not fail."

Barak followed Deborah's battle plan. Sisera's forces were defeated. None survived, except for Sisera, who ran to the tent of Jael where he hid under a blanket. While Sisera was sleeping, Jael pounded a tent stake through his head and showed Barak her handiwork when he arrived. As Deborah predicted, the final victory was in the hands (and the hammer) of a woman.

When it was all over, Deborah and Barak celebrated the victory with a song (Judges 5:1-31) that scholars generally consider to be one of the oldest pieces of literature in Scripture. Deborah became one of the most heroic, if easily overlooked, figures of biblical history.

The question is: What on earth (literally, *on earth*) do followers of Jesus do with a story like this? How do followers of the "Prince of Peace" deal with a story that is soaked in bloodshed, violence, and war?

This is the kind of story that causes many thoughtful people to reject the Old Testament. People who are reading the Bible for the first time are sometimes shocked and often turned off by the sheer amount of bloodshed and violence in the Hebrew Scriptures and the way much of it is seemingly commanded by God.

In response, the first thing we can do is name it: There is a lot of violence in the Old Testament. God's relationship with Israel was revealed in a world that operated on the assumption that might makes right and that a nation's favor with God was confirmed by its military power. God's covenant with Abraham was hammered out in a sin-broken, war-torn, politically conflicted, power-intoxicated world that was not all that different from the world in which we live.

The second thing we can do is remember that these stories were not the firsthand accounts of a CNN reporter on the scene. The Hebrew people told and retold these stories for generations after the events as a way of putting their history into the context of the covenant. As a result, they were not interested in answering a lot of the questions we are interested in asking. They were not historians doing academic research. They were cultural theologians who interpreted everything that happened in light of their covenant relationship with God.

Finally, as followers of Jesus, we can read these stories from the perspective of the gospel. We can interpret these stories through the Word made flesh in the words and way, the life, death, and resurrection of Jesus.

When we do that, we begin to see the violence in these stories as a fundamental contradiction of the nonviolent kingdom of God revealed in Jesus Christ; the Kingdom, we pray, will come on earth as it is in heaven. Conflict, bloodshed, and war are never God's will. There is no such thing as a "holy" war. Rather, we can read these stories as the all-too-graphic evidence of the persistent power of sin. Violence between nations and people is the result of our sinful rebellion against the saving, life-giving purpose of God.

It is possible that our discomfort with these stories is a sign that we are getting closer to the heart of the gospel. The more intimately we follow Jesus, the more difficulty we have with the violence in these stories, the conflict in our world, and the hostility in our own hearts and lives.

During the struggle against apartheid in South Africa, Methodist pastor Trevor Hudson led his white congregation on what came to be known as "The Pilgrimage of Pain and Hope" as a way of building relationships with black South Africans. It was not an easy journey. One day his daughter asked, "Why do you follow Jesus when he keeps getting you into so much trouble?"

The more closely we follow Jesus, the more deeply we engage in the values of the kingdom of God, the more we find ourselves out of sync with many of the assumptions of the conflict-ridden culture in which we live.

How might the story of Deborah speak to us today?

By an interesting twist of Providence, I was scheduled to preach on Deborah on the Sunday prior to the Fourth of July. As I reflected on the Song of Deborah in that context, I began to think that the Hebrew people repeated Deborah's story and sang her song in a way that was similar to the way American citizens recite Longfellow's version of "The Midnight Ride of Paul Revere."

Both poems contain details that are difficult to reconcile with what we know of the historical event. Their purpose was not historical analysis but to awaken people from their lethargy. The Hebrews passed Deborah's story on to awaken their faith, stir their conscience, call them to action, and remind them of their identity as the covenant people of God.

In the same way, Longfellow concluded the legend of Paul Revere's ride with a challenge to his readers.

> For, borne on the night-wind of the Past,
> Through all our history, to the last,
> In the hour of darkness and peril and need,
> The people will waken and listen to hear
> The hurrying hoof-beats of that steed,
> And the midnight message of Paul Revere.

Deborah aroused her people to go to war. Unfortunately, we had more than enough of that call in the decade following the 9/11 attacks; and the world has paid an awful price for it.

Perhaps we need the spirit of Deborah to arouse us to what the pilgrims called "the common good." We need Deborah to remind us that our individual freedoms are bound up in what the preamble to the Constitution called "the general welfare." My freedoms are restrained by my responsibility to others in my community and nation.

We need the voice of Deborah to awaken us to values that are wider than narrow self-interest, higher than the lowest common denominator of rampant individualism, and noble enough to lift us out of the paralysis of political polarization by uniting us in a fresh vision of who we are and who we have it in us to become.

That is what Abraham Lincoln did at Gettysburg. Historians tell us that the ground was soggy with the shallow graves of the dead from both North and South. The air hung heavy with the stench of decaying bodies when Lincoln delivered the 273 words that historian Garry Wills called "The Words That Remade America."

Lincoln reminded a war-torn nation of the common roots out of which we had come. "Four score and seven years ago our fathers brought forth on this continent, a new nation, conceived in Liberty, and dedicated to the proposition that all men are created equal."

He named the horrendous cost of our conflict. "We cannot dedicate—we cannot consecrate—we cannot hallow—this ground. The brave men, living and dead, who struggled here, have consecrated it, far above our poor power to add or detract."

In perhaps the greatest understatement in American history, he said, "The world will little note, nor long remember what we say here, but it can never forget what they did here."

He concluded with words that continue to arouse us from our lethargy and call us to go forward with the unfinished work we have to do. "It is for us the living, rather, to be dedicated here to the unfinished work which they who fought here have thus far so nobly advanced. It is rather for us to be here dedicated to the great task remaining before us . . . that this nation, under God, shall have a new birth of freedom—and that government of the people, by the people, for the people, shall not perish from the earth."

The truth is that there are times when we become discouraged or downhearted. The issues we confront and the struggles we face sometimes seem to overwhelm us. In those times, we need the Spirit of the God who spoke through Deborah to awaken us from our lethargy and to energize us for the still unfinished work we have to do.

# QUESTIONS

1. What was the purpose of the Lord giving the Israelites over to King Jabin of Canaan in verse 2? What do we learn in verse 3 about the technological superiority of the Canaanites?

2. The Hebrew words translated "wife of Lappidoth" in verse 4 can also be translated "woman of torches." Is this an accurate descriptor of Deborah? Why or why not?

3. Deborah was the only named female leader (judge) of Israel and the only named prophet in Judges. What circumstances do you think led to such an unusual appointment to a leadership position for a woman during this time period?

4. In verse 6, why does Deborah word her question to Barak in such a way? Why does Barak refuse to go into battle unless Deborah goes as well?

5. In verse 9, Deborah tells Barak that the LORD is going to hand Sisera over to a woman. Does this play out the way you expected? Why, or why not?

6. In verse 19, why does Jael give Sisera milk to drink when he asks her for water?

7. Were Jael's actions in verses 17-22 faithful and heroic or deceitful and sinful? Give reasons for your response.

8. Compare and contrast Deborah and Jael. In what ways are they both exceptional among biblical figures?

9. In Judges 5:7, Deborah is called "a mother in Israel," the only biblical figure to be given this descriptor. In what ways was Deborah a mother in Israel?

10. What qualities of leadership are exemplified by Deborah? What can Christians today learn about leadership by reading this passage?

# 2

# ABIGAIL
## TOO WISE FOR WAR

## SCRIPTURE
### 1 SAMUEL 25:1-44

¹Now Samuel died, and all Israel gathered to mourn for him. They buried him at his home in Ramah. David then left and went down to the Maon wilderness.

²There was a man in Maon who did business in Carmel. He was a very important man and owned three thousand sheep and one thousand goats. At that time, he was shearing his sheep in Carmel. ³The man's name was Nabal, and his wife's name was Abigail. She was an intelligent and attractive woman, but her husband was a hard man who did evil things. He was a Calebite.

⁴While in the wilderness, David heard that Nabal was shearing his sheep. ⁵So David sent ten servants, telling them, "Go up to Carmel. When you get to Nabal, greet him for me. ⁶Say this to him:

'Peace to you, your household, and all that is yours! [7]I've heard that you are now shearing sheep. As you know, your shepherds were with us in the wilderness. We didn't mistreat them. Moreover, the whole time they were at Carmel, nothing of theirs went missing. [8]Ask your servants; they will tell you the same. So please receive these young men favorably, because we've come on a special day. Please give whatever you have on hand to your servants and to your son David.'"

[9]When David's young men arrived, they said all this to Nabal on David's behalf. Then they waited. [10]But Nabal answered David's servants, "Who is David? Who is Jesse's son? There are all sorts of slaves running away from their masters these days. [11]Why should I take my bread, my water, and the meat I've butchered for my shearers and give it to people who came here from who knows where?" [12]So David's young servants turned around and went back the way they came. When they arrived, they reported every word of this to David.

[13]Then David said to his soldiers, "All of you, strap on your swords!" So each of them strapped on their swords, and David did the same. Nearly four hundred men went up with David. Two hundred men remained back with the supplies.

[14]One of Nabal's servants told his wife Abigail, "David sent messengers from the wilderness to greet our master, but he just yelled at them. [15]But the men were very good to us and didn't mistreat us. Nothing of ours went missing the whole time we

were out with them in the fields. [16]In fact, the whole time we were with them, watching our sheep, they were a protective wall around us both night and day. [17]Think about that and see what you can do, because trouble is coming for our master and his whole household. But he's such a despicable person no one can speak to him."

[18]Abigail quickly took two hundred loaves of bread, two skins of wine, five sheep ready for cooking, five seahs of roasted grain, one hundred raisin cakes, and two hundred fig cakes. She loaded all this on donkeys [19]and told her servants, "Go on ahead of me I'll be right behind you." But she didn't tell her husband Nabal.

[20]As she was riding her donkey, going down a trail on the hillside, David and his soldiers appeared, descending toward her, and she met up with them. [21]David had just been saying, "What a waste of time—guarding all this man's stuff in the wilderness so that nothing of his went missing! He has repaid me evil instead of good! [22]May God deal harshly with me, David, and worse still if I leave alive even one single male belonging to him come morning!"

[23]When Abigail saw David, she quickly got off her donkey and fell facedown before him, bowing low to the ground. [24]She fell at his feet and said, "Put the blame on me, my master! But please let me, your servant, speak to you directly. Please listen to what your servant has to say. [25]Please, my master, pay no attention to this despicable man Nabal. He's exactly what his name says he is! His name means fool, and he is foolish! But I myself, your servant,

didn't see the young men that you, my master, sent. [26]I pledge, my master, as surely as the Lord lives and as you live, that the Lord has held you back from bloodshed and taking vengeance into your own hands! But now let your enemies and those who seek to harm my master be exactly like Nabal! [27]Here is a gift, which your servant has brought to my master. Please let it be given to the young men who follow you, my master. [28]Please forgive any offense by your servant. The Lord will definitely make an enduring dynasty for my master because my master fights the Lord's battles, and nothing evil will be found in you throughout your lifetime. [29]If someone chases after you and tries to kill you, my master, then your life will be bound up securely in the bundle of life by the Lord your God, but he will fling away your enemies' lives as from the pouch of a sling. [30]When the Lord has done for my master all the good things he has promised you, and has installed you as Israel's leader, [31]don't let this be a blot or burden on my master's conscience, that you shed blood needlessly or that my master took vengeance into his own hands. When the Lord has done good things for my master, please remember your servant."

[32]David said to Abigail, "Bless the Lord God of Israel, who sent you to meet me today! [33]And bless you and your good judgment for preventing me from shedding blood and taking vengeance into my own hands today! [34]Otherwise, as surely as the Lord God of Israel lives—the one who kept me from hurting you—if you hadn't come quickly and met up with me, there wouldn't be one single male left come morning." [35]Then David accepted everything she

had brought for him. "Return home in peace," he told her. "Be assured that I've heard your request and have agreed to it."

[36]When Abigail got back home to Nabal, he was throwing a party fit for a king in his house. Nabal was in a great mood and very drunk, so Abigail didn't tell him anything until daybreak. [37]In the morning, when Nabal was sober, his wife told him everything. Nabal's heart failed inside him, and he became like a stone. [38]About ten days later, the LORD struck Nabal, and he died.

[39]When David heard that Nabal was dead, he said, "Bless the LORD, who has rendered a verdict regarding Nabal's insult to me and who kept me, his servant, from doing something evil! The LORD has brought Nabal's evil down on his own head." Then David sent word to Abigail, saying that he would take her as his wife.

[40]When David's servants reached Abigail at Carmel, they said to her, "David has sent us to you so you can become his wife."

[41]She bowed low to the ground and said, "I am your servant, ready to serve and wash the feet of my master's helpers." [42]Then Abigail got up quickly and rode on her donkey, with five of her young women going with her. She followed David's messengers and became his wife.

[43]David also married Ahinoam from Jezreel, so both of them were his wives. [44]But Saul had given his daughter Michal, David's wife, to Palti, Laish's son, from Gallim.

# INSIGHT AND IDEAS

There's only one way to say this. Abigail was a very wise woman with a very foolish husband. Her husband's name was Nabal, the Hebrew word for "fool" or "foolish man."

While doing online research about Abigail, I found some fascinating sermon titles that capture something of her story. One was "Just Because You Live With a Fool Doesn't Mean You Have to Be One." My favorite was "What to Do When You're Married to a Jerk."

Like the foolish man in one of Jesus' parables, Nabal was very rich. The Book of First Samuel introduces him as "a very important man [who] owned three thousand sheep and one thousand goats." Nabal was clearly among what we would call the 1 percent.

The writer draws the contrast by saying that Abigail was "an intelligent and attractive woman, but her husband was a hard man who did evil things."

Enter David, who was not yet king and was hiding out in the wilderness with a ragtag gang of rejects and ruffians waiting for his chance take Saul's throne. He sent messengers to remind Nabal that while his sheep were grazing in the fields, David's men had protected them from attack. Not unlike "The Godfather," now that it was sheepshearing time, David was sending his thugs to collect protection money.

In addition to being rich and foolish—or perhaps because of it—Nabal was also arrogant. He sneers at David's messengers, "Who is David? Who is Jesse's son? . . . Why should I take my bread, my water, and the meat I've butchered for my shearers and give it to people who came here from who knows where?"

David's knee-jerk reaction to Nabal's insult is to call out his troops. "Then David said to his soldiers, 'All of you, strap on your swords!' So each of them strapped on their swords, and David did the same."

Both Mark Twain and Abraham Maslow are credited with saying that if all you have is a hammer, everything looks like a nail. David's reaction is all too often the knee-jerk reaction of powerful people, powerful leaders, and powerful nations in our sin-twisted, violence-addicted, conflict-prone world. When we are hurt or offended, when our position, pride, or power are threatened, our first reaction is to hit back, strap on the sword, or fire up the drones.

I'm convinced that one of the most obvious signs of the persistent power of sin is the way we continue to believe in the age-old myth of redemptive violence. We believe against the evidence that we can resolve resentments with violence, bring reconciliation by force, and make peace through war. Like David, our knee-jerk reaction is to strap on a sword.

We can feel David's red-hot anger when he says, "May God deal harshly with me, David, and worse still if I leave alive even one single male belonging to him come morning!"

David not only resorted to violence, but to violence that was totally out of proportion to the offense. He went way beyond the Old Testament restriction of "an eye for eye, tooth for tooth." He took four hundred men and headed off to kill Nabal and all his men.

One of Nabal's servants caught wind of the attack and pleaded with Abigail, "See what you can do, because trouble is coming for our master and his whole household. But he's such a despicable person no one can speak to him" (verse 17).

That's when Abigail's womanly wisdom kicked in. While the men in the story were ready to bludgeon each other, Abigail looked for another solution. Without telling her dolt of a husband, she loaded up the donkeys with bread, wine, butchered sheep, grain, and fig cakes and headed out to find David.

When they met, Abigail delivered one of the longest speeches of any woman in Scripture in which she told David, "Pay no attention to this despicable man Nabal. He's exactly what his name says he is! His name means fool, and he is foolish!" (verse 25). That's her husband she's talking about!

With the wisdom of a political consultant, Abigail warned David that his action in the present could have a negative impact on his future. "When the Lord has done for my master all the good things he has promised you, and has installed you as Israel's leader, don't let this be a blot or burden on my master's conscience, that you shed blood needlessly or that my master took vengeance into his own hands" (verses 30-31).

Her words changed David's mind and reversed the direction of the story. David responded, "Bless the LORD God of Israel, who sent you to meet me today! And bless you and your good judgment for preventing me from shedding blood and taking vengeance into my own hands today! Otherwise, as surely as the LORD God of Israel lives—the one who kept me from hurting you—if you hadn't come quickly and met up with me, there wouldn't be one single male left come morning" (verses 32-34).

Abigail returned home to find Nabal in a drunken stupor. When he sobered up the next morning, she told him what happened. He collapsed with a heart attack and within ten days was dead. David took Abigail as the second of his eight wives and when he ruled as king, she was at his side.

Aside from advising women not to marry a drunken fool regardless of how rich he is, what does Abigail have to teach us?

First, Abigail's story reminds us of the folly of resorting to violence and the wisdom of searching for a nonviolent way to resolve conflicts. It's foolish to follow the world's way of violence and wise to find God's way of reconciliation and peace.

What we have here are two proud, powerful men who are headed toward war until a wise woman finds another way to resolve their conflict. Just because she was married to a fool didn't mean she had to be one.

Second, Abigail is a woman who, at great risk to herself, did what she could to resolve the conflict. With absolutely no assurance that her action would make any difference, she did what she could and trusted the outcome to God.

I'll grant that Abigail is a minority character in the Old Testament. There is more than enough violence in the Old Testament, much of it supposedly done in the name of God. But here in the early pages of our spiritual history is an otherwise powerless woman who had the wisdom to confound the foolishness of the men around her by seeking to find God's way of reconciliation and peace. Abigail's actions point toward the day when Jesus would say that you can pick out the people who represent the Kingdom of God because they love their enemies and do good to those who persecute them. "Happy are people who make peace," Jesus said, "because they will be called God's children" (Matthew 5:9).

As it was in Abigail's story, this kind of godly wisdom usually comes from outside the places or systems of power. It is often a minority opinion and more often than not it is rejected by the powerful majority. But it lives on as the relentless witness of God's wisdom that calls us to the way of reconciliation and peace.

When it comes down to it, a disciple of Jesus Christ chooses Jesus' way of nonviolence and peacemaking, not because there is any guarantee that it will "work" by the world's standards, because it often doesn't; not because it is a quick fix to long-term bitterness, resentments, and conflict, because it isn't; and not because it is a politically expedient position to take, because it never will be. Followers of Jesus choose his way of reconciliation and nonviolence solely because they are convinced that it is the way Jesus lived and it is the way he expects his disciples to live.

Rose Whiteside was a contemporary Abigail in our congregation. Your first impression would be that she was a loving grandmother who worked in her garden and studied her Bible. She was both of those things, but if you thought that was all there was to Rose, you had a big surprise coming.

Rose took Jesus seriously when he called his followers to be active as peacemakers. She did what she did because she really believed that this is what Jesus expects his followers to be doing. That was enough.

On Christmas Day 2003, instead of going over the river and through the woods to their grandchildren's house, Rose and her husband, Haven, boarded a plane that took them to Baghdad, where they served for five weeks as members of a Christian Peacemaker Team.

The local daily newspaper ran a feature on the Whitesides' trip to Iraq, noting that the couple would be spreading the message of Christmas—peace on Earth and good will toward all—to a war-torn country. Haven Whiteside explained their rationale for taking such a risk: "'We go there to live a Christian life, and that means following what Jesus said: `Love your enemies.'"

Some of the couple's friends and family questioned the wisdom of their decision. One son's immediate response was, "You're stupid!" But his mother simply laughed and reasoned, "You have to answer that call when you get it. . . . We have people who are committed to war. Why shouldn't we be committed to peace and be willing to take risks for peace?"

Rose and Haven lived outside the safety of the "Green Zone" among ordinary Iraqi people. They helped families navigate the information maze to track down their missing relatives. They visited and prayed with military personnel. They did what they could to be the living presence of a peace-filled alternative to the violence that surrounded them.

Some people thought that Rose and Haven were foolish. I suspect that people thought that Abigail was foolish, too. But it turned out to be foolish wisdom that saved the day. It was, in fact, the foolishness that would later be revealed at a cross, the foolishness that Paul said "is wiser than human wisdom . . . stronger than human strength" (1 Corinthians 1:25).

May God be at work in the conflicted relationships of our lives, in the hostility of our conflicted culture, and in this blood-soaked, violent world, to make us, like Abigail, the instruments of peace.

# QUESTIONS

1. What is the significance of the passage's contrast of Abigail with her husband, Nabal, in verse 3?

2. Did David have a right to be so angry with Nabal? Why, or why not?

3. How important is Nabal's servant (verse 14) to the outcome of this story?

4. Why is Abigail able to talk David "off the ledge"? How did she show wisdom? What might she have done differently?

5. How might David and Abigail's futures have been different if David had taken his revenge unrestrained?

6. Why does David marry Abigail? What are the similarities and differences between this story and the account of David and Bathsheba in 2 Samuel 11?

7. Abigail's speech (verses 24-31) is one of the longest speeches by a woman recorded in Scripture. Why, do you think, was it included?

8. In what ways does this passage indicate that Abigail could be considered to be serving as a representative for God?

# 3

# MARY MAGDALENE
## THE FIRST APOSTLE

## SCRIPTURE
### MATTHEW 27:55-61; 28:1-10

### MATTHEW 27:55-61

[55]Many women were watching from a distance. They had followed Jesus from Galilee to serve him. [56]Among them were Mary Magdalene, Mary the mother of James and Joseph, and the mother of Zebedee's sons. [57]That evening a man named Joseph came. He was a rich man from Arimathea who had become a disciple of Jesus. [58]He came to Pilate and asked for Jesus' body. Pilate gave him permission to take it. [59]Joseph took the body, wrapped it in a clean linen cloth, [60]and laid it in his own new tomb, which he had carved out of the rock. After he rolled a large stone at the door of the tomb, he went away. [61]Mary Magdalene and the other Mary were there, sitting in front of the tomb.

### MATTHEW 28:1-10

[1]After the Sabbath, at dawn on the first day of the week, Mary Magdalene and the other Mary came to look at the tomb. [2]Look, there was a great earthquake, for an angel from the Lord came down from heaven. Coming to the stone, he rolled it away and sat on it. [3]Now his face was like lightning and his clothes as white as snow. [4]The guards were so terrified of him that they shook with fear and became like dead men. [5]But the angel said to the women, "Don't be afraid. I know that you are looking for Jesus who was crucified. [6]He isn't here, because he's been raised from the dead, just as he said. Come, see the place where they laid him. [7]Now hurry, go and tell his disciples, 'He's been raised from the dead. He's going on ahead of you to Galilee. You will see him there.' I've given the message to you."

[8]With great fear and excitement, they hurried away from the tomb and ran to tell his disciples. [9]But Jesus met them and greeted them. They came and grabbed his feet and worshipped him. [10]Then Jesus said to them, "Don't be afraid. Go and tell my brothers that I am going into Galilee. They will see me there."

# INSIGHT AND IDEAS

We can blame Pope Gregory the Great for giving Mary Magdalene a bad reputation. In 591 he outed her as the unnamed prostitute who broke open an alabaster jar of priceless ointment, poured it on Jesus' feet, and dried them with her hair. Here's what Gregory said:

"It is clear, brothers, that the woman previously used the unguent to perfume her flesh in forbidden acts."

You have to give Gregory credit for having a sensuous imagination. Jesus said of that woman, "Her many sins have been forgiven; so she has shown great love. The one who is forgiven little loves little" (Luke 7:47).

That story appears in Luke's Gospel just before he introduces us to Mary Magdalene (Luke 8:2). It's a questionable reason for linking the two women, but it stuck in the Christian imagination for a long time.

In the twelfth century, Bernard of Clairvaux established "Magdalene houses" to rescue women from prostitution. The tradition comes down to us in imaginatively inaccurate novels such as *The DaVinci Code* and pathos-packed movies such as *The Passion of the Christ*. It's on Broadway in the revival of *Jesus Christ Superstar*. Evidently, imagining Mary as a sinner is more interesting than following her as a saint.

But Mary has been in rehab lately. In 1969, the Vatican finally rejected Gregory's linkage of Mary with the sinful woman in Luke's Gospel. In 1988, Pope John Paul II observed the obvious, that Mary and the other women were the first witnesses to the resurrection. He described Mary with a tenth-century title, *apostola apostolorum,* "the apostle to the Apostles."

Recently there's been a faddish fascination with second- and fourth-century texts known as the Gnostic Gospels, including one known as the Gospel of Mary along with a tiny fragment of text that some have suggested hints that Jesus had a wife. Bypassing all of the hype, there is enough in the Gospels to confirm this definition of discipleship from the current pope.

"The story of Mary of Magdala reminds us all of a fundamental truth. A disciple of Christ is one who, in the experience of human weakness, has had the humility to ask for his help, has been healed by him and has set out following closely after him, becoming a witness of the power of his merciful love that is stronger than sin and death."[1]

When we look at what Luke's Gospel says about Mary, we begin to see her as the down-to-earth model of what it looks like to be a disciple of Jesus Christ. Luke introduces her to us as being one of the women who traveled with Jesus and the disciples. "Among them were Mary Magdalene (from whom seven demons had been thrown out), Joanna (the wife of Herod's servant Chuza), Susanna, and many others who provided for them out of their resources" (Luke 8:2-3).

There's no real value in speculating about the medical or psychological condition that Luke described as demonic possession. In fact, leaving it undefined leaves space for us to find ourselves in her story.

---

1 Catholic News Agency, July 22, 2012. <http://www.catholicnewsagency.com/saint.php?n=309> [accessed January 3, 2013]

The point is that Mary was an imperfect, hurting, broken human being, just like all of us, who, in Pope Benedict's words, "had the humility to ask for his help"; who found healing, wholeness, and new life in Jesus; and who, in response to what Christ had done in her life, followed him and gave of her resources to support Jesus' mission.

Mary reminds us that being a disciple of Jesus Christ involves having the humility to acknowledge that we are imperfect, broken, sinful people who desperately need the forgiveness, grace, and healing that only Christ can give. To be a disciple is to receive that healing and give ourselves away in extravagant gratitude for what Christ has done in our lives.

Lois was a small woman with great strength who faced some very difficult times in her life. When she told her story, she would say that there came a time in her life when she gave up trying to do it on her own, turned it over to Christ, and allowed him to make something beautiful of her life. In planning for her memorial service, she instructed that the soloist sing Bill Gaither's "Something Beautiful," a stirring song that describes a broken life that has been redeemed through Christ.

That's what happened for Mary. That's what happened for Lois. That's what happens for every disciple of Jesus Christ. As a result, Mary followed Jesus all the way to the cross, followed him all the way to the tomb.

If we try to put ourselves into the story, the burden the Gospel writers place on men is that they ran away. The blessing the Gospel writers place on women is that they stayed. The Gospels agree that Mary Magdalene and the other women were with Jesus when they nailed him to the cross. They were there when Joseph of Arimathea took his bloody, battered body down from the cross. They were with him all the way to the tomb.

Mary demonstrates a fundamental truth about being a disciple, the hard truth that the purveyors of pop religion don't want you to know. Sooner or later, following Jesus means following him to a cross. The process of dying and rising again is not a one-time event that happened to Jesus. It is the basic pattern of our discipleship.

Jesus made this point clear when he said, "Unless a grain of wheat falls into the earth and dies, it can only be a single seed. But if it dies, it bears much fruit. . . . Whoever serves me must follow me" (John 12:24-26). With disturbing consistency, Jesus said that anyone who wants to be his disciple will have to deny his or her own self-interest, take up a cross, and follow him.

Sooner or later, every disciple will come to times and places where they are called to surrender some old attitude, old prejudice, old habit, old way of thinking and living so that they can experience the new life Christ has to give and become a part of the coming of his Kingdom in this world. It's what Paul was talking about when he said, "I have been crucified with Christ and I no longer live, but Christ lives in me" (Galatians 2:20).

The seventeenth-century Anglican priest and later Baptist preacher Thomas Shepherd asked the question in a hymn:

> Must Jesus bear the cross alone,
> And all the world go free?
> [And he gave what would have been Mary's answer.]
> No, there's a cross for everyone,
> And there's a cross for me.

The journey leads to Mary's greatest scene in the Gospel drama when she and the other women were the first people to see the empty tomb. Mary became the first witness to the risen Christ. There, at the empty tomb, she received her apostolic commission from the angel who said, "Hurry, go and tell his disciples, 'He's been raised from the dead. He's going on ahead of you to Galilee. You will see him there.' I've given the message to you" (Matthew 28:7).

A few moments later, she received the same commission from Christ himself. "Don't be afraid. Go and tell my brothers that I am going into Galilee. They will see me there" (Matthew 28:10).

Mary Magdalene became the *apostola apostolorum*, "the apostle to the Apostles." She heard the command to "Go and tell." And that's exactly what she did.

That same apostolic commission comes to every disciple of the risen Christ. Benedict got it right when he said that the fundamental truth Mary teaches us about being a disciple is that we become "a witness of the power of his merciful love that is stronger than sin and death."

Not long ago I visited with a woman who reminded me a lot of Mary. She knows how it feels to be a broken, imperfect person. She knows what it means to experience the healing, forgiveness, and grace that only Christ can give. Like Mary, she gives herself away as an expression of her love for Christ.

She knows how it feels to follow Jesus to the cross, to that place where she surrendered part of herself in order to follow him. She knows the power of the risen Christ at work in her life. And she said to me, "I can't wait for other people like me to experience the love of God the way I've found it in this church."

Like Mary, she has received the apostolic commission to "go and tell" what Christ has done in her life.

So, where are you in this story? You may be at a place where you need to acknowledge that you are a broken, imperfect, sinful person who needs the forgiving grace and the healing love that only Christ can give. Mary invites you to receive.

You may sense that it is time for you to take your next step in following Jesus, even when it leads to a cross, to that place where you allow old ways of thinking and living to die so that new life can be born. Mary invites you to follow.

You may have experienced new life of the risen Christ and now it's time for you to hear Jesus say, "Go and tell." Mary, the apostle to the Apostles, challenges you to take the good news to someone else.

# QUESTIONS

1. Why, do you think, does Mary Magdalene so capture the imaginations of many Christians when they read the gospels?

2. Why were Mary Magdalene and the other two women in Matthew 27:55-56 watching the Crucifixion "from a distance"?

3. On the evening when Jesus was buried, why were Mary Magdalene and the other Mary sitting in front of the tomb after the stone was rolled into place (Matthew 27:61)? Why, do you think, does the Scripture include this detail?

4. Why did Jesus choose to appear first to Mary Magdalene and the other Mary after his resurrection?

5. Matthew 28:9 tells us that when Jesus appeared to the two women, they "grabbed his feet and worshipped him." Why is this significant?

6. In Matthew 28:10, Jesus tells the two women not to be afraid, but to go and tell the others that he's alive and going to Galilee. Why did Jesus tell them not to be afraid?

7. Luke 8:2 tells us that seven demons had been expelled from Mary Magdalene. Why, do you think, does the Bible share this detail?

8. Why is Mary Magdalene known to many Christians as "the first apostle"?

9. What can we learn from Mary Magdalene about discipleship and sharing the gospel?

# 4

# THE SAMARITAN WOMAN
## WHERE TO GO WHEN YOU
## REALLY NEED A DRINK

## SCRIPTURE
### JOHN 4:4-42

[4]Jesus had to go through Samaria. [5]He came to a Samaritan city
called Sychar, which was near the land Jacob had given to his son
Joseph. [6]Jacob's well was there. Jesus was tired from his journey,
so he sat down at the well. It was about noon.

[7]A Samaritan woman came to the well to draw water. Jesus said
to her, "Give me some water to drink." [8]His disciples had gone into
the city to buy him some food.

[9]The Samaritan woman asked, "Why do you, a Jewish man, ask
for something to drink from me, a Samaritan woman?" (Jews and
Samaritans didn't associate with each other.)

[10]Jesus responded, "If you recognized God's gift and who is saying to you, 'Give me some water to drink,' you would be asking him and he would give you living water."

[11]The woman said to him, "Sir, you don't have a bucket and the well is deep. Where would you get this living water? [12]You aren't greater than our father Jacob, are you? He gave this well to us, and he drank from it himself, as did his sons and his livestock."

[13]Jesus answered, "Everyone who drinks this water will be thirsty again, [14]but whoever drinks from the water that I will give will never be thirsty again. The water that I give will become in those who drink it a spring of water that bubbles up into eternal life."

[15]The woman said to him, "Sir, give me this water, so that I will never be thirsty and will never need to come here to draw water!"

[16]Jesus said to her, "Go, get your husband, and come back here."

[17]The woman replied, "I don't have a husband."

"You are right to say, 'I don't have a husband,'" Jesus answered. [18]"You've had five husbands, and the man you are with now isn't your husband. You've spoken the truth."

[19]The woman said, "Sir, I see that you are a prophet. [20]Our ancestors worshipped on this mountain, but you and your people say that it is necessary to worship in Jerusalem."

[21]Jesus said to her, "Believe me, woman, the time is coming when you and your people will worship the Father neither on this mountain nor in Jerusalem. [22]You and your people worship what you don't know; we worship what we know because salvation is from the Jews. [23]But the time is coming—and is here!—when true worshippers will worship in spirit and truth. The Father looks for those who worship him this way. [24]God is spirit, and it is necessary to worship God in spirit and truth."

[25]The woman said, "I know that the Messiah is coming, the one who is called the Christ. When he comes, he will teach everything to us."

[26]Jesus said to her, "I Am—the one who speaks with you."

[27]Just then, Jesus' disciples arrived and were shocked that he was talking with a woman. But no one asked, "What do you want?" or "Why are you talking with her?" [28]The woman put down her water jar and went into the city. She said to the people, [29]"Come and see a man who has told me everything I've done! Could this man be the Christ?" [30]They left the city and were on their way to see Jesus.

[31]In the meantime the disciples spoke to Jesus, saying, "Rabbi, eat."

[32]Jesus said to them, "I have food to eat that you don't know about."

[33]The disciples asked each other, "Has someone brought him food?"

[34]Jesus said to them, "I am fed by doing the will of the one who sent me and by completing his work. [35]Don't you have a saying, 'Four more months and then it's time for harvest'? Look, I tell you: open your eyes and notice that the fields are already ripe for the harvest. [36]Those who harvest are receiving their pay and gathering fruit for eternal life so that those who sow and those who harvest can celebrate together. [37]This is a true saying, that one sows and another harvests. [38]I have sent you to harvest what you didn't work hard for; others worked hard, and you will share in their hard work."

[39]Many Samaritans in that city believed in Jesus because of the woman's word when she testified, "He told me everything I've ever done." [40]So when the Samaritans came to Jesus, they asked him to stay with them, and he stayed there two days. [41]Many more believed because of his word, [42]and they said to the woman, "We no longer believe because of what you said, for we have heard for ourselves and know that this one is truly the savior of the world."

# INSIGHT AND IDEAS

She came to the well at high noon. Unlike the rest of the women who came in the morning or the evening, she came in the heat of the day. And unlike the other women, she came alone.

She was a social outcast, a woman with a bad reputation. The respectable women in the village didn't like her and my guess is that she didn't like the way they looked down their self-righteous noses at her. That may be why she came at noon and came alone.

The well was not only the place where the women of the community came to draw water; it was also the gathering place where single men came to find a wife. That's how it worked out for Isaac, Jacob, and Moses in the Old Testament. "Give me something to drink" was evidently an ancient Middle Eastern "pick-up line." If a woman dropped her bucket into the well, you knew where this story was going.

This woman had been to that well before. Six times, in fact, she had dropped her bucket into the well and every time it came up empty as the men in her life used and abused her.

When I think of this woman, I remember Fantine's pain-soaked song in the Broadway musical *Les Misérables*. There was a time when she dreamed that love was blind, that men were kind, that their voices were inviting, and that God would be forgiving. She dreamed of a time when hopes were high and life was worth living. But then it all went wrong. She remembered the man who slept a summer by her side but was gone when autumn came. Life had killed the dream she dreamed.

That's how I picture this woman. Along with her empty bucket, she carried with her the emptiness of her broken dreams; the pain of her shattered hopes; and an inescapable thirst for one who would love her rather than use her, one who loved her for who she was and not for what he could take from her.

That's when she noticed a single man waiting at the well. John says that Jesus was there because he was tired. I take great consolation in knowing that Jesus got tired—tired of the people pressing in on him, tired of the work of ministry. I'm glad that Jesus got tired, because I get tired, too. That's why he was there.

The woman, however, had every reason to assume that he wanted something else. Even worse, she could see that he was a Jew.

The parenthetical note in verse 9 contains one of the great understatements of Scripture: "Jews and Samaritans didn't associate with each other." Behind that statement were four centuries of ethnic prejudice, religious bigotry, and social segregation. It's no wonder that when Jesus asked for a drink, she shot back, "Why do you, a Jewish man, ask for something to drink from me, a Samaritan woman?"

The same question comes down to us across all the long, sad history of prejudice, bigotry, and segregation.

Why would you, a well educated, upwardly mobile white man ask a drink of me, a poor, marginalized, black woman?

Why would you, a Northerner, ask a drink of me a guy from the South?

Why would you, so obviously straight, ask a drink from me, just as obviously gay?

Why would you, a conservative Republican, ask a drink of me, a liberal Democrat?

The labels change, but the social separation remains the same through all of the fractured relationships with which we live.

That's when Jesus turned a pick up line she was ready to reject into an invitation she couldn't refuse. It was, in fact, an offer of incalculable love and grace. "If you recognized God's gift and who is saying to you, 'Give me some water to drink,' you would be asking him and he would give you living water."

Like so many conversations in John's Gospel, this is a classic of missed communication. Their words simply bypass each other. She's thinking literally, calculating the depth of the well and the impossibility of drawing water without a bucket. Jesus is talking figuratively, using the metaphor of "living water" to describe the Spirit of God so deeply at work within us that is like a spring of water, not imposed from without, but bubbling up within the human soul. It's the biblical metaphor that runs from the garden in Genesis to John's image in Revelation of a day when no one will be thirsty again. She's thinking water; he's thinking Spirit. She's talking about the well and the bucket; he's talking about her heart and soul.

But something about the water Jesus offered and something about the way he offered it touched that arid place
in this woman's broken soul. With a transparency that she
had never risked before, she said, "Sir, give me this water, so
that I will never be thirsty and will never need to come here
to draw water!"

Have you noticed how difficult it is for most of us to acknowledge our spiritual thirst? Years ago I saw a cartoon
out of *The New Yorker* in which two camels were standing
in the scorching heat of an arid desert. One was saying to
the other, "I don't care what anyone says, I'm thirsty."

It's often difficult to name the thirst in our lives, to identify
the broken place in our lives. Sometimes we hide behind a
protective veneer of pride and social acceptability rather
than tell the truth about ourselves. But this woman was
ready to acknowledge that she was thirsty for the water
that only Jesus could give.

Like a skillful cardiologist going carefully to the damaged
place in her heart, Jesus said, "Go, get your husband, and
come back here." Something in the way Jesus said it made
her feel as if she could trust him with the deepest hurt, the
darkest pain, the most devastating disappointment in her life.

She said, "I don't have a husband." She had had men and
they had had her, but she had not had someone who
really loved her. Jesus told her that she had spoken the
painful truth that was at the bottom of the relentless thirst
in her soul.

That was when she knew that the one to whom she was speaking was the one for whom she had always been waiting; the one who would really love her; the one who loved her enough to enter into the deepest, most painful truth in her life. In opening that thirst to Jesus, she found living water, not drawn from the well, but bubbling up in her own soul. She left her water jar behind; went back to the people who had rejected her; and told them all, "Come and see a man who has told me everything I've done! Could this man be the Christ?"

In John's Gospel, "Come and see" is the recurring invitation for each person to check Jesus out for himself or herself. Don't miss the way the woman left the people with a question that they alone would have to answer. They came and saw and John records that "Many more believed because of his word, and they said to the woman, 'We no longer believe because of what you said, for we have heard for ourselves and know that this one is truly the savior of the world'" (John 5:41-42).

What a story! What a woman! And John didn't even catch her name.

I've heard and preached many sermons on this story. They usually focus on what this story tells us about Jesus. That is, after all, what John intended. He wrote, "These things are written so that you will believe that Jesus is the Christ, God's Son, and that believing, you will have life in his name" (John 20:31). But I'm fascinated with this woman.

She came to the well broken, empty, and dying of thirst.

She met Jesus and opened her broken dreams to him in transparent vulnerability.

Rising up within her soul she discovered a life-giving, healing water that she wasn't able to draw from the well.

She went out to invite the very people who had marginalized her to "come and see."

And because of her witness, they found that living water for themselves. My guess is that life around that old well was never quite the same again.

It still happens. When the church is really the church, it's the kind of place where we are drawn into relationship with people with whom we would never have had anything in common. It's a place where people who by the world's standards are separated from each other are drawn together in the love of Christ.

I'll never forget Esther. She was one of the first people I met when I came to Hyde Park twenty years ago. She was a tough, strong-willed woman. Raised in the Deep South, she was the first woman to receive a law degree from Emory University, but she was basically unreconstructed when it came to race. The first time we recognized Martin Luther King Sunday by singing "We Shall Overcome," she let me know in no uncertain terms that it was something she did not appreciate.

You can imagine her surprise when she went to the first session of Disciple Bible Study and discovered a black woman sitting across the table from her. It wasn't easy; but after more than thirty-four weeks of living together with Scripture, they became friends. When Esther died, that same woman bore witness to their love for each other and sang at her funeral.

It still happens. When the church really is the church, it's the kind of place where broken lives are made whole. A woman in our congregation told me that she identified with the woman at the well. The details of their stories are radically different, but the end result was the same: shattered dreams, deep pain, and an arid soul. It felt as if the dreams she dreamed had died.

In that desert place, she opened her brokenness to the love of God and to the love of other followers of Jesus in our congregation. She's on the journey toward wholeness and healing. She told me that because she talks so openly about her experience, she is afraid people will think she is in a rut. In what must have been a gift of wisdom from the Spirit, I found myself saying, "You know, a rut becomes a river when fresh water flows through it."

Because this woman allowed both Jesus and her friends to walk with her through that desert place, we have tasted the living water that bubbles up like an ever-flowing stream through the broken places in her life.

If the Samaritan woman were telling her story today, my guess is that she would ask us, "Is anybody thirsty?" My guess is that she would offer the invitation, "Come and see a man who told me everything I've ever done." And perhaps we would join her in singing words of Psalm 107:

> "Give thanks to the LORD because he is good,
>    because his faithful love lasts forever!"
>    . . .
> Some of the redeemed had wandered into the desert,
>        into the wasteland.
>    They couldn't find their way to a city or town.
> They were hungry and thirsty;
>    their lives were slipping away.
> So they cried out to the LORD in their distress,
> and God delivered them from their desperate circumstances.
>    . . .
> Let them thank the LORD for his faithful love
>    and his wondrous works for all people,
>        because God satisfied the one who was parched with thirst.
>    . . .
> God can also turn the desert into watery pools,
>    thirsty ground into watery springs.

## QUESTIONS

1. Why was it considered shocking for Jesus to initiate an encounter with the Samaritan woman at the well?

2. Why doesn't Jesus correct the woman when she continues to think that he's talking about physical water?

3. Why does Jesus seemingly change the subject in verse 16? Why does the woman change the subject in verse 20?

4. How might the woman's answer in verse 17 be considered factually correct but misleading at the same time?

5. Why doesn't Jesus directly deal with the issue the woman raises in verse 21? What does it mean to worship God in spirit and truth?

6. How does Jesus' conversation with the disciples about food and harvests relate to the encounter with the Samaritan woman?

7. What can modern Christians learn from the Samaritan woman about doing effective evangelism? What can we learn from Jesus?

8. How are our lives shaped by public perception? How did Jesus restore the Samaritan woman's life and reputation?

9. In what ways does this Bible passage offer hope to "outsiders"?

10. What is the significance of what the Samaritans said in verse 42? Why is this concept important for evangelism today?

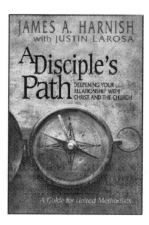
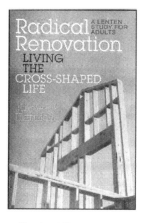

# CONVERGE

## Bible Studies

### OUR COMMON SINS
by Dottie Escobedo-Frank
9781426768989

### WHO YOU ARE IN CHRIST
by Shane Raynor
9781426771538

### SHARING THE GOSPEL
by Curtis Zackery
9781426771569

### KINGDOM BUILDING
by Grace Biskie
9781426771576

And more to come.

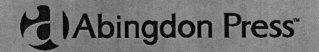

CPSIA information can be obtained at www.ICGtesting.com
Printed in the USA
BVOW03s1445300314

349136BV00010B/112/P

9 781426 771545